Palmetto Publishing Group
Charleston, SC

A Capitol Dream
Copyright © 2019 by Emilie Kefalas

First Edition

Printed in the United States

ISBN-13: 978-1-64111-366-3
ISBN-10: 1-64111-366-9

A CAPITOL DREAM

EMILIE KEFALAS

Emilie gets ready for her first day as a tour guide at the United States Capitol Building.

She memorizes the architects, the rooms, and every detail so she knows exactly what to say.

When Emilie opens her eyes, she discovers she's at work and her first tour is about to start!

She scans the room to find none other than George Washington waiting patiently for a tour guide.

"Good morning sir! My name is Emilie and I'll be your Capitol tour guide."

"It's a pleasure to meet you, Miss Emilie. I'm George Washington, but please, call me General."

5

They take the elevator to the tunnel floor. "We are now in the tunnels, a series of underground hallways connecting the Capitol, the Library of Congress, and the Senate and House office buildings," Emilie explained.

They enter the U.S. Capitol Visitor Center, a giant underground room where visitors enter the Capitol Building.

There are many large statues in the room.

"I've noticed that on these statues are the names of different territories. Why is that?" Mr. Washington asks.

"Each state donates two statues of people who are very important to the history of that state," she says.

"How many statues
are there?"
Mr. Washington asks.

"One-hundred.
Two from every state."

9

They come across a statue of a man with a parchment in his fist. It belongs to the District of Columbia, as in Washington, D.C.

The statue is of Frederick Douglass.

As Emilie and Mr. Washington look at the plate on which his name is listed, Mr. Douglass suddenly steps down from his podium.

"Excuse me," he begins, "is this where I join the tour of the Capitol?"

"Yes sir! My name's Emilie and this is-"

"Mr. President, it's an honor," Mr. Douglass says extending his hand to Mr. Washington.

"Mr. Douglass, the honor is all mine. Please join us."

They approach a large marble statue.

"Notice this one does not belong to a state," Emilie says.

Mr. Washington and Mr. Douglass observe the statue, a woman wearing a helmet and holding a shield and sword.

13

The General asks, "Is she Liberty?"

"She is the symbol of Liberty. Her official name is Freedom. This is a plaster model of the bronze version atop the Capitol dome."

"If I recall correctly," Mr. Douglass begins, "she was assembled with the help of a slave during the Civil War."

"You're absolutely right, Mr. Douglass," Emilie says. "His name was Philip Reid. He was freed in April of 1862 when President Abraham Lincoln signed the Compensated Emancipation Act. How fitting this plaster model of the statue he helped create resides here in Emancipation Hall."

They continue to a round-shaped room with many columns.

"The room is called the Crypt. Built in 1793, it is the oldest room in the Capitol," Emilie explains.

"Ah yes, I remember as if it were yesterday I was asked to lay the cornerstone of the Capitol here," Mr. Washington exclaims. "It was rather heavy since it was made of sandstone."

17

"This room was originally designed as a tomb, but no one is actually buried here or anywhere in the Capitol," she explains.

Mr. Washington asks, "Who was supposed to be laid to rest here?"

"Well . . . you were," Emilie answers.

Mr. Douglass walks over to one of the columns. "Are these bullet holes? From the War of 1812?"

"You're right, Mr. Douglass," Emilie says. "The British attacked the Capitol in 1814. See over there? There's a huge burn mark from where they tried to set the building on fire. Thankfully, they were unsuccessful."

19

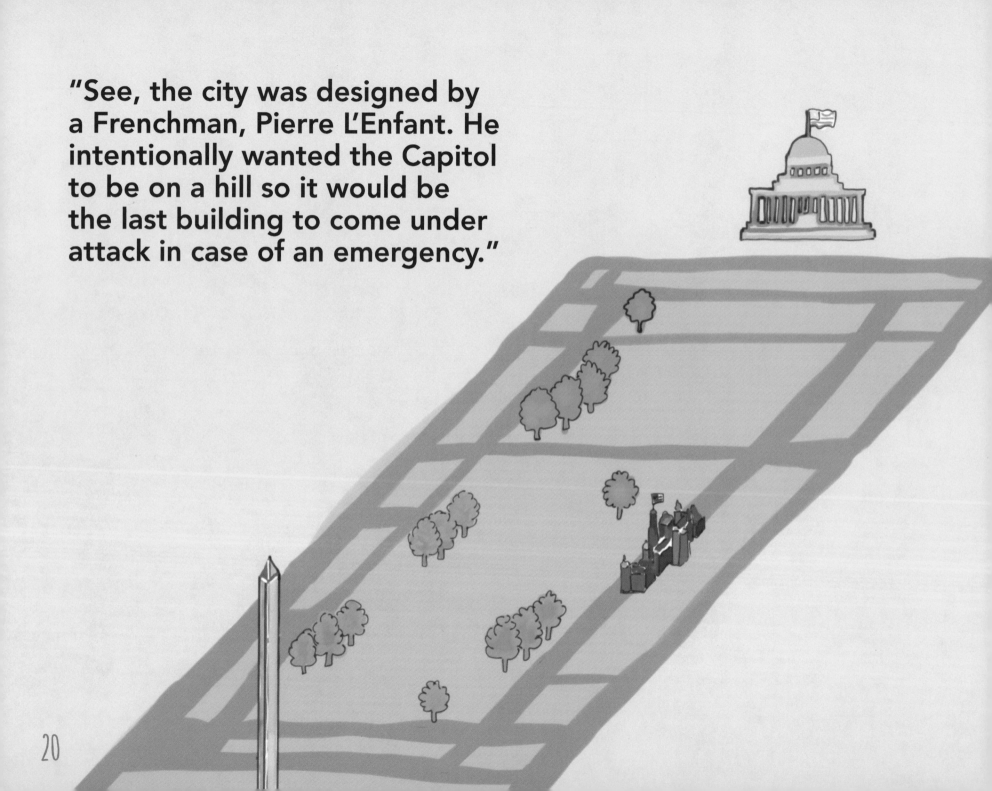

"See, the city was designed by a Frenchman, Pierre L'Enfant. He intentionally wanted the Capitol to be on a hill so it would be the last building to come under attack in case of an emergency."

Out through the Crypt, Emilie leads Mr. Washington and Mr. Douglass quickly through the Hall of Columns.

"There are 28 columns lining this hallway," she explains. "Some of the state sculptures in here are among my favorites in the Capitol."

She proceeds to point out two very different figures.

The first one is a marble statue of a young man with a rifle at his feet.

"Here we have Stephen Austin, the founder of the state of Texas."

They walk a little further down and stop near a bronze statue of a man with a cane.

"This is Father Damien of Hawaii, a Saint and servant to the poor and sick who himself had leprosy."

"Miss Emilie, this statue looks different from Mr. Austin's," Mr. Washington observes. "Who sculpted these? I can't imagine a single sculptor, no matter how skilled, could live long enough to create all 100 statues."

"I'm glad you brought that up, General," Emilie says.

"Many of the 100 statues, including these two I just showed you, were sculpted by female artists.

A French artist named Marisol Escobar sculpted Father Damien's statue, and a German-American sculptor named Elisabet Ney created Mr. Austin's."

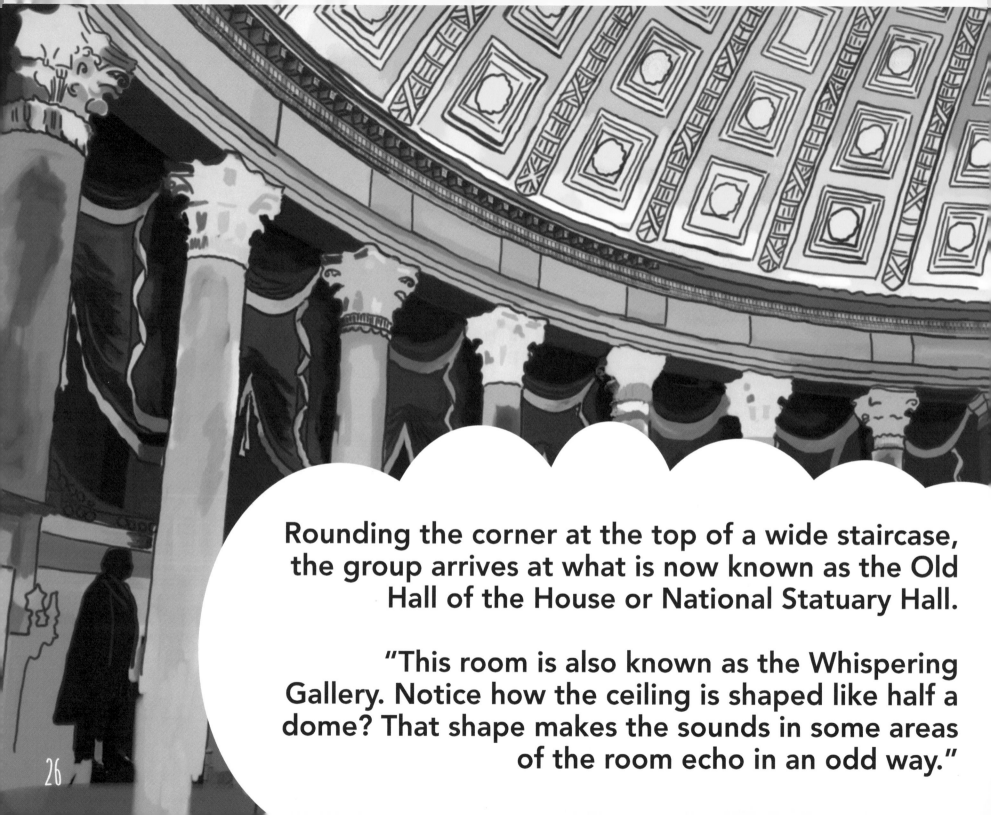

Rounding the corner at the top of a wide staircase, the group arrives at what is now known as the Old Hall of the House or National Statuary Hall.

"This room is also known as the Whispering Gallery. Notice how the ceiling is shaped like half a dome? That shape makes the sounds in some areas of the room echo in an odd way."

26

"Oh my word," Mr. Washington says, looking at a floor tile across the room. "I believe this is John Adams's boy, John Quincy."

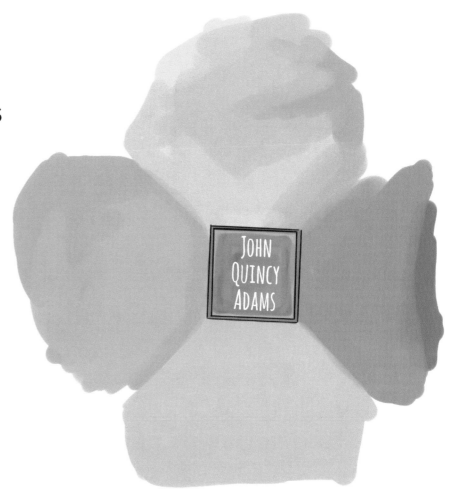

JOHN QUINCY ADAMS

"If you stand near Mr. Adams's tile," Emilie says, "anything you say will echo across the other side of the room."

Emilie then leads Mr. Washington and Mr. Douglass through the Capitol Rotunda.

"This is remarkable," Mr. Douglass says.

They stand in the center of the Rotunda near a small bronze circle on the floor.

"All around us are scenes from our country's history," Emilie says as she points to a series of paintings encircling the Rotunda's lower walls.

"They show different events during the United States' growth from an unexplored land to a democracy."

The gentlemen look up at the "Apotheosis of Washington" on the Rotunda ceiling. It depicts Mr. Washington surrounded by thirteen maidens representing the thirteen original colonies.

Suddenly, Emilie feels a tap on her shoulder. She turns around to see . . Elizabeth Cady Stanton.

"Pardon me, ma'am," Miss Stanton begins. "I overheard you describing the details of this room, and I thought I'd introduce myself. I'm Elizabeth Cady Stanton. My sculpture is over there." She points to a marble sculpture with three busts, including hers, carved in it.

"Thank you for joining us, Miss Stanton. This is General George Washington and Mr. Frederick Douglass."

Miss Stanton shakes hands with both gentlemen.

"We've met," Mr. Douglass says.

"This is the Portrait Monument," Emilie explains. "From right to left, we have Lucretia Mott, Susan B. Anthony, and you, Miss Stanton. This sculpture is dedicated to the pioneers of the Woman Suffrage Movement, which won women the right to vote in 1920."

"I'm very proud to be immortalized in such a way alongside such remarkable women," Miss Stanton says, gazing at the Portrait Monument.

33

"You know what I love about this room," Emilie asks. "It represents America's diverse origins."

"It makes me very happy," Mr. Washington remarks, "to see young people like you, Miss Emilie, keeping these stories alive."

Just as Emilie is about to reply, her tour group begins to look blurry. In fact, everything in the room slowly fades away...

Emilie's alarm clock buzzes. Her eyes open. It's 6:30 a.m.

It's time to get ready for her first "official" day as a Capitol tour guide!

Emilie takes the metro to Capitol Hill a few minutes early.

She sips her coffee and gazes at the Capitol dome.
Freedom stands as tall and as proud as ever.

"I can do this. I won't be alone,"
she says to herself.

"HISTORY WILL BE WALKING WITH ME."

39

Revisit the U.S. Capitol with Emilie at ACapitolDream.com.

And for more Capitol adventures, follow @acapitoldream on Instagram and Facebook!

40

Photo by Nazli Flores.

41

Photo by Nazli Flores.

ABOUT THE AUTHOR

Emilie Kefalas is a writer and avid history buff from Decatur, Illinois (the Soybean Capital of the World).

She was introduced to the history of the U.S. Capitol when she served as a congressional intern for her home district's congressman. As an intern, one of her favorite duties was leading constituents on tours of the Capitol Building.

In an effort to share her passion for both U.S. history and giving tours, Emilie created this illustrated guide for young constituents to use during their Capitol visits and beyond.

43

CPSIA information can be obtained at www.ICGtesting.com
Printed in the USA
BVIW121144180120
569930BV00014B/372